Motivational Energy

Julie Graham-Tremillo

Dedication:

I dedicate this book to my family, with thanks for all of their patience, support, understanding, encouragement, and inspiration.

Special thanks go to my husband, Antonio Tremillo, and to my kids.

Special thanks to my sister Tammy, who helped with editing, and to my daughter Ella, who helped with designing my cover.

Each person in my family has contributed to this book in some way, whether they knew it or not.

I love you all, with every bit of Energy that I have within myself.

Table of Contents:

Introduction

Energy and motivation have always fascinated me. I knew that there was a connection between the two, but it took me a while to figure out what it was. In this book, I discuss mostly motivation, but I have tried to tie into it the energy behind the motivation.

Everything has energy. Every living thing, every person, plant, animal, all have energy. Inanimate objects also have energy. That's basic science. The atoms in an object are constantly vibrating. Inanimate objects, such as a table, have a slower vibration. The atoms don't move very much or very far apart, but they are still vibrating. Therefore, they have energy. Vibration is energy.

It is easier to sense the energy in people, more so than anything else. We have different ways of communicating that allow us to get that energy message across. Aside from speaking, we have body language, and tone of voice. Sometimes, people don't even have to speak for you to be able to feel their energy.

Have you ever been in a situation where someone walks in the room and you can just sense their mood? Maybe they are angry and you can feel the tension. Or maybe they are bubbling with happiness and you can feel that energy too.

Positive people tend to give off positive energy, while negative people tend to give off negative energy. Of course nobody is either completely positive or completely negative.

We tend to react to each other's energy. In fact, we often feed off of each other's energy. You have friends that come to you when they are down? How does that affect you? Do they leave you feeling better or worse? If when they leave, they feel better and you feel worse, they have probably fed off of your energy. They needed positive energy to balance themselves, so they took yours.

If you have energy to spare, that's no big deal, as you can always replenish yourself. Positive energy ultimately comes from one source and that is God, or your Heavenly Father, or the Universe, or the Universal Source of Power….whatever you want to call

Him. When you are able to connect directly with that Universal Source, you can replenish yourself. Other people, who do not know how to connect to that Source, have to steal energy from other people in order to replenish themselves.

Energy motivates us. Without energy, we are just plodding through life, just getting by. But if we are able to find our source of energy, we become motivated. We work harder to connect with that energy. Then that energy motivates us to do more.

Motivational energy is what keeps our world progressing. If nobody was ever motivated to do anything, we would still be living in caves. Luckily, someone was motivated to figure out how to start that first fire so that we could learn how to cook our food.

We are far from knowing all of the secrets of the universe. What if there are more secrets out there that are just as important as fire? Shouldn't we always be motivated towards seeking more?

In this book, I want to help you learn what motivates you. I want you to understand the different types of motivation and why you are motivated to do things that other people are not. I want to help you learn to set goals in your life and work every day towards obtaining that goal.

We all have things in life that we want to do. If we don't, we certainly should. In this book, I want to help you to discover what those things are that you want to do. I also want to help you to accomplish them. I want to help you to analyze your life and your personality and target the reason why you may not be getting the things done in your life that you want to get done. I want to help you decide to do something, whether it is starting on a new job, career, or education, a new goal in your life, a new relationship ….whatever goal it is, I want to help you identify that goal and work towards attaining that goal by first changing yourself from the inside. Let's get started.

Motivation

Do you ever wonder why it seems like some people are just super motivated towards their goals and other people seem to have no goals at all and are motivated towards nothing? Don't you just sometimes wish that you could motivate people to do something with their lives? Whether it's your kids, your family, your friends, your co-workers or your employees, there is probably somebody that you have tried to motivate at some point.

Do you ever just sit there and shake your head and say, "I just don't get it, why won't they do this?" Or "It's not that hard, if they would just do this...."

It helps if you understand motivation. There are different types of motivation: intrinsic and extrinsic, positive and negative. We will go over each kind and discuss combinations.

Intrinsic motivation is often called self-motivation. Self-motivation is the most powerful form of motivation. Self-motivation will make you get out of bed an hour before you have to because you are ready to face the day and get started on your tasks. Self motivation is what is going to make you want to spend your evenings learning something new or doing extra work instead of vegging out in front of the TV night after night.

Extrinsic motivation is when you are motivated by an external force.

Someone pays you to do something, so you are motivated to do it. That is also positive extrinsic motivation. Someone yells at you, so you are motivated. That is extrinsic negative motivation. Your mother-in-law is coming to visit, so you clean your house. All of these are examples of extrinsic motivation. Extrinsic motivation is not nearly as powerful and long lasting as intrinsic motivation. Yes, extrinsic motivation will get the job done sometimes. But self-motivation is what will get the job done right and on a regular basis.

There is also positive and negative motivation. Positive and negative motivation comes from positive and negative energy. Positive energy tends to motivate you to do positive things. Negative energy, though, can be dangerous. While it is possible for negative energy to motivate you to do positive things, it is more likely to motivate you to do negative things. So when you have negative motivational energy, you really have to be careful of which direction you are going in. For example, if you become angry, you develop a negative energy. That energy can be used for good or bad. If you become angry and that makes you go do something productive, like decide to go to college because you are so angry at your situation or mildly angry, so you clean your whole house to release that energy, that is an example of when negative energy is used productively in a positive manner.

But if you become angry and start plotting your revenge...that is when it negative energy is producing negative results. (Unless your revenge is to go to college and "show them"). When you plot against someone in order to hurt them because you are angry, that is when negative energy is producing negative results.

Everything has energy. People, plants, animals, even inanimate objects all have energy.

"Energy" is neither good nor bad, but it is positive and negative. It is what you choose to do with that energy that is good or bad. I have used negative energy a lot in my life to produce positive results. For the longest time, the only kind of energy that I had was negative energy. Then I figured out that positive energy is more effective than negative energy and it doesn't zap all of my energy when I am using it.

With negative energy, you burn it off until it is gone, and then you are drained, because you were trying to get rid of that negative energy. But positive energy, even though it can be draining….you tend to be able to build on that. It is much healthier for you, and doesn't leave you with a headache and feeling deflated.

Sometimes all of these forms of motivation can work together. People who are intrinsically motivated to do their work because they get a sense of accomplishment and feel good about themselves may also be extrinsically motivated because someone pays them to do that work. This can be a touchy area.

Sometimes people start doing the work just because they are paid to do the work. They may then lose their sense of intrinsic motivation. They will no longer be self motivated to do the work and it then becomes more of a "job".

But then there are others who continue to do the same work in the same manner because they enjoy the work, they get that sense of accomplishment, and they feel good about a job well done. The money is nice, but they would still do the work with the same degree of passion, no matter how much they are paid.

If a person is intrinsically motivated to do something, offering them more money to do it is not going to make them motivated to do it better. They will still put forth the same effort that they always did.

However, a person who is extrinsically motivated to do the work may actually improve the quality of their work if they are offered more money to do it, at least temporarily.

Since intrinsic motivation is the most powerful and longest lasting form of motivation, wouldn't it be nice if we could just MAKE everyone intrinsically motivated? Yes, that would be nice. Unfortunately, it doesn't work that way. You cannot MAKE someone intrinsically motivated. By the very definition of the word, it is impossible.

Intrinsic motivation has to come from within a person. It is a fire burning within them that must be quenched.

You cannot force it, but you can foster it. You can encourage it and inspire It. Your job here is to make them want to do the work.

Foster intrinsic motivation

Acknowledging other people helps foster intrinsic motivation. When you see them doing something right, tell them what a good job they are doing. So often, accomplishments go unnoticed. When that happens, people often get discouraged and may lose the desire to do well. So when your kids or your employees, or anyone else does a good job or a good thing, let them know that they did well. Let them see that you noticed and that you appreciate what they did.

Encourage people to do things on their own. Encourage them to try new things. Even if they get it wrong, or it's not exactly how you would do it, encourage them. When they are done, don't sit there and point out everything that they did wrong. When you do that, it makes them not want to try next time. Point out everything they did right. If you must point out what is wrong, make sure to balance it with positive comments. A good rule of thumb is this: for every negative comment you say, balance it with at least 3 positive comments. Make sure they are genuine. People know when you are faking it. Kids know.

Give examples. When people see a physical example of what they are supposed to do, they can look at it and visualize how it works. They don't have to reinvent the wheel. They can look at this example that you give them and decide ways to improve upon it. In this way, you have inspired intrinsic motivation.

Physical examples work well when it is something PHYSICAL that you want someone to work on. But what about when it's not a physical thing? What about when it's a character trait, or something else that you can't see and touch? When that happens, use role models.

Role Models

It's important to have good role models, whether you are a child or adult. So often, as adults, we forget that we need role models. We get caught up in our daily lives and never really think about needing a role model.

Your kids probably have role models without even realizing it; people on TV or computer, maybe their teachers or other students. Whether they are good role models or bad role models, they have them. Talk to your kids about role models and find out who theirs are. Don't be offended if they don't consider you a role model.

Kids often choose superheroes as a role model. That's okay. They need heroes. But talk to them and find out what traits they admire in those superheroes. Most superheroes have a few things in common: honesty, respect for others, friendliness, service to others. They help the "little guy" and contribute to their community. Most likely your kids won't point out all those characteristics, so it's up to you to do that. If you want to be your child's role model, you have to model those traits. Eventually, as your child gets older, they will see those same superhero traits in you.

Adults need role models too. Consider carefully who you choose for a role model. Think about the characteristics that you admire most. Think of who you want to be like, or what character traits you would like to have. Maybe you will have several different role models for different character traits that you want to have. Find those role models and then study their lives. Figure out how they got to where they are.

I have role models, but those people don't even realize it. In fact, I don't even know most of them. But I study their lives and read their books and in that way, I feel like I know them well enough that they can be my role models. I think of them as a "council" where they sit around this table and I can go to them with problems and get their opinions.

Your parents are natural role models to you, from the time you are born. That can be good or bad, depending on your parents. With mine, I take the good character traits and use those as a model, but I leave the bad. So while I still consider them role models, I acknowledge that they have faults and there are certain characteristic traits that I would not like to follow.

When I was little, I was a very shy, passive person. No matter what anyone said or did to me, I would not argue or resist in any way. I would just accept it. I felt like I didn't have a right to an opinion. I thought that other people's opinions mattered more than mine. What I needed or wanted wasn't as important as what other people needed or wanted. I took what was given to me and I didn't ask for anything else because I was afraid I would be told no.

I studied the other kids. I tried to figure out what I was doing wrong. But I couldn't figure it out. I would talk to my sisters. They would tell me to just "be yourself." I remember thinking that was a really bad idea because people didn't like me.

I wish now that I would have had someone sit down and explain to me why I was like that. If I could go back in time, I would go back and talk to a younger version of me. I would explain to her what passive is. I would tell her how to overcome being passive.

A Word About Bullying

I was bullied quite a bit when I was little. I was normally the smallest, the shyest, and the poorest. I was an easy target. I don't remember ever crying, though. I probably did. I just don't remember it. I went inside of myself where people couldn't hurt me. I withdrew from everything around me. I had no real friends, except in my mind. And in my mind, I had great friends. I was a completely different person inside my mind. I saw the word around me. I saw what was happening. But I chose not to participate in it.

Normally, I had a running commentary in my mind, constantly analyzing what was going on around me. I wasn't really emotionally involved in anything though.

I was extremely passive. I was labeled as shy, and I was shy. But something inside of me, that "other me" was confident and assertive. I just needed to find a way to bring that part of me into the real world.

I didn't understand this at the time, of course, but I learned later in life that there are three types of people: Assertive, Passive, and Aggressive.

People who are assertive are less likely to be bullied. They are also less likely to bully other people. In order to understand "assertiveness," we must also understand "passive" and "aggressive."

These character traits are sometimes easier to define in kids, but they apply to adults as well. In this program, we mostly focus on kids and how to help them overcome problems such as passiveness and aggression. Many of our suggestions focus on parental involvement. However, the same concepts will apply to adults.

Passive means that you accept or allow whatever is happening without resisting. It means that, whatever happens, right or wrong, you don't fight against it. You don't try to change it. You just accept it.

Aggressive means that you are ready to attack, even when there is nothing to attack. Can also mean that you are on the defensive.

Assertive means that you are confident, bold, and decisive.

Passive

A passive person is very likely to become depressed. They have wants and needs, but they don't express them. They don't think that their opinion is important or they are afraid that other people will ridicule them. But how did that person become passive to begin with? Maybe they are modeling the behavior of others around them. If their parents are passive, they are more likely to be passive. If their ideas are constantly criticized and they are not encouraged to make decisions on their own, they are more likely to be passive. If they are always told "no" when they ask for things that they need or want, they can become passive. Parents should be careful of this. You don't want to give your child everything that they ask for, because then they don't learn how to handle it when someone tells them "no." But you also don't want to always tell them "no." If every time they ask you for help or a toy or a certain food, you always tell them "no," they will learn to not ask for what they want or need. They will already know the answer, so they won't bother asking.

Passive people tend to wait for people to notice that they need something. They don't ask for what they want or need. If they are insulted, they don't resist or defend themselves. They don't stand up for themselves or other people.

Passive people often feel like they are being taken advantage of. They feel like their opinions are not acknowledged and they feel like they don't get credit for their own ideas. They may feel resentment or anger. They are not confident. They keep their feelings locked inside, which causes a lot of their depression. They often feel helpless and hopeless to change anything.

They underestimate the value of their own opinions. They worry about what other people will think of them. They are afraid of voicing their own opinions because they think others will reject them or think they are stupid.

A passive person is extremely sensitive to criticism, even "constructive criticism." They often lose hope or give up when faced with any opposition or criticism. A negative comment can affect their whole day or even week.

Aggressive

Aggressive people are more likely to become bullies. They tend to think that their opinions and their wants and needs are more important than other people's. They push people to do things that they don't want to do. They often talk down to other people. They can be condescending. They belittle people. All of these negative actions that they perform towards other people help them to feel better about themselves.

It is very common for aggressive people to have a sort of false confidence. They project a confident attitude, but they are not really confident. A truly confident person has no need to belittle or insult other people.

Aggressive people often use guilt to manipulate people into doing what they want them to do. They make other people feel bad and don't respect other people's wishes, opinions, or desires. They often use sarcasm as a weapon, lashing out at other people in an effort to make themselves seem more important or smarter.

Aggressive people are often able to get people to do things because they bully them into doing it. However, those people who are doing things for them end up angry and resentful because their opinions and desires were not respected. They will then lose respect for the aggressive person and the aggressive person will lose friends.

Some causes of aggression are:

- Focusing on themselves instead of others

- Not learning to respect other people or value their opinions

- Not learning how to truly listen

- Mimicking behavior of those around them, including friends or parents

Assertive

Assertive people are the healthiest and happiest, and normally most successful people. They are less likely to be bullied and they are less likely to bully other people. Assertive people respect other people's rights, desires, and opinions. They do not have to insult other people in order to make themselves feel better. They speak up for their rights and the rights of others. When they want something, they go after it. They ask for what they want or need.

Assertive people are confident and bold. They are direct. They don't "beat around the bush." When they want something, they don't hint about it, but rather, they come right out and say it.

Assertive people believe in themselves. They believe that their opinion matters and the opinions of other people matter. They believe that they have a right to express their opinions and desires. They respect other people and their opinions.

Learn to be assertive

Anybody can learn to be assertive. Even if you are naturally aggressive or naturally passive. You can learn to be assertive and retrain yourself. Look at other people. See if you can tell who is passive, who is aggressive, and who is assertive. Find people who are assertive and notice the differences in them in comparison to other people. Do they have more friends? Do they tend to get what they want? Do people like them?

If you are naturally passive, you probably can't just jump right in to being assertive and think that you can do it right the first time. People may not respond to you the way that you think they should.

You have to take baby steps. Start small. Don't just expect to be able to get up in front of a crowd of people and be confident and assertive if you haven't been practicing.

Start with smaller things. Make small decisions and make your opinions known. Start with those closest to you, such as your close friends and family. Explain to them that you are trying to learn to be more assertive because you believe that you will be happier and healthier. Ask for their help. Ask them to gently point out when you are being passive.

If you are teaching your kids to be assertive, start by giving them small things to do. Encourage them to ask the waitress for another drink instead of asking for them. Encourage them to make decisions and solve their problems on their own. But let them know that you will be available to help them if they need help. Making these small decisions and learning to solve their own problems will help them become more confident and more assertive.

Have an opinion

It is very easy for a passive person to just not have an opinion. Sometimes they have to dig a little deeper into themselves to find their opinion. They are so used to other people making the decisions for them that they just stop making decisions and stop having opinions.

So if you are passive, HAVE AN OPINION and voice it. When someone asks you what you want for dinner, have an opinion and voice it. Notice how many times you say, "I don't know, what do you want?" How many times do you pass the decision making on to someone else? Unless you genuinely do not care about what you are eating for dinner, have an opinion.

When we always let other people make the decisions, we aren't always happy with the results. We may even start to resent the other person who makes those decisions for us. We think that they don't care about what we want, which isn't true because otherwise they wouldn't ask questions like what we want for dinner.

You don't have to wait for them to ask. Just voice your opinions, your needs, and your wants. You can't just sit around expecting other people to notice that you have a problem. That won't always happen. If they notice, that's great. But don't expect it.

It is not their job to take care of your problems. It is not their job to figure out what you need. It is YOUR JOB to take care of your problems. It is your job to voice your needs and wants.

You are responsible for your own happiness

It is your job to make yourself happy. You are responsible for your own happiness. True happiness is intrinsic. That means that it comes from within you. It does not come from an external force. Although certain external things may cause temporary happiness, true long lasting happiness must come from within ourselves. We have to look within our hearts and see what makes us happy. If you are happy, those around you are more likely to be happy. However, please realize that other people's happiness is not your responsibility. I know, right? That completely goes against what you were raised to believe! At least it did for me. This was a shocking fact for me....other people's happiness is not your responsibility. It is their responsibility to make themselves happy. It is not your job to make your kids happy. It is not your job to make your spouse happy. That is their responsibility.

Happiness is intrinsic. It comes from within ourselves. We cannot "make" someone else happy. They have to do that for themselves. Yes, there are things that we can do that will temporarily make them happy, but that is not a lasting, long-term happiness.

When your kids are little, you try to "make" them happy. You give them what they want and you think they are happy. And they are, temporarily. But they have to learn to be happy without someone giving them things and without someone doing things for them. They have to learn true inner peace in order to be truly happy.

That's what you can help them with. You can help them learn to be at peace within themselves. You can teach your kids to meditate. You can encourage them to spend time away from electronics. You can encourage them to spend more time in nature. You can teach them to love silence. How can they really "hear" what is inside of their heads and their hearts if they are never silent? Teach them to calm the chatter that runs constantly through their minds. When they learn that, they will be on the road to learning how to be truly, intrinsically happy.

Don't expect so much from other people. Don't expect other people to "make" you happy. That is not their job. They cannot do it long term. It is your job to learn to make yourself happy. It is unfair of you to expect other people to make you happy. Especially since they cannot really do it.

Look inside of yourself

Look inside of yourself and see your inner beauty. See the good that is inside of you. Other people don't always see the good inside of you because you keep it hidden. Think about all of the things you are good at. Maybe you are nice to your sister. Maybe you help your mom. Maybe you are good at organizing. There are things that you are good at. Focus on those things.

Don't focus on the things that you are not good at. Identify what you are not good at, but don't focus on it. Acknowledge when you are not good at something. Come up with solutions to fix each problem. Deal with facts only. Don't make the problem bigger than it is. Don't get overly emotional about a problem and blow it out of proportion. Focus only on the facts. You have to deal with your emotions and reactions to the facts separately.

Stay Positive

Use positive self talk. Those are the thoughts that are always running through your head. If those thoughts are always negative, they will make you feel bad about yourself. You will become withdrawn and depressed. Other people will see that you are withdrawn and depressed, and they won't want to have anything to do with you.

I covered this in depth in my one of my other books, "The Power of Positivity." If you have a problem with negative self talk, please read that book.

Self talk can make or break us. If we are constantly saying nice, positive things to ourselves, our actions will be good and positive. But if our self talk is always negative, so will be our actions.

When we think positively and act positively, other people behave differently towards us. They behave more positively towards us. I call this a "bounce back affect." Whatever we project, that is what gets bounced back at us. So if we are always frowning at people, they are likely to frown at us. But if we are smiling at people, they are more likely to smile at us.

Nobody is perfect

Remember that nobody is perfect. Sometimes we look at other people and everything we see seems perfect. But we are not seeing the whole picture. We aren't seeing what they don't want us to see. Maybe they just don't do the things that they are not good at.

Concentrate on what you are good at. Focus on that. But remember to always try new things. With practice, you will get better. If you know that you are not good at something and you don't try to improve it, you probably will not magically get better at it. So, if it is important to you, practice it. But if it is something that you actually don't care about, don't feel like you have to be good at it just to make other people happy. Practice what YOU want to be good at.

Try new things. If you are interested in something, try it, study it, and learn how to do it. Figure out what you are passionate about. When you find it, do it. Practice it until you are good at it. We always do better when we are passionate about it. Learning to do more things will help you become more confident.

Expect the best of people

Expect people to be good. If you think highly of them, they will act better. If you brag on your kids, and tell them what good people they are and what a great job they are doing, they will act better all the time. But if you go around telling everyone that your kids are bad and they have bad manners and they never behave, your kids will be bad and have bad manners and never behave. Make them think highly of themselves and they will act better. Build their confidence so that they know they are capable.

Confidence

Build your confidence through positive self talk. Stop telling yourself that you are stupid and that you do everything wrong. I have seen this so often. People come into my shop and say, "I am so stupid. I don't know how to do this…." They are their own worst enemy. They tell themselves over and over that they are stupid. They convince themselves that they are unworthy. If they are telling me that they are stupid, how much more critical of themselves are they when they are alone?

It has become a way of life for them, this constant negative self talk. If you always tell people that you are stupid, they will start to believe it and they will treat you like you are stupid.

Is it any wonder that your personal relationships suffer?

If you are confident, you will be able to handle situations better. You will be able to be more assertive. Stop talking bad about yourself. Stop doubting yourself. You don't know everything, nobody does. You have to learn, just like everyone else. You can learn anything. You can do ANYTHING that you set your mind to. The limitations exist only in your mind. Stop making excuses. You are capable.

Start by talking positive to yourself. Turn negative statements into positive statements.

Instead of "I am too stupid for this," say "I don't know how to do this, but I can learn."

Tell yourself how awesome you are. It's not being conceited; it is building your confidence. "Wow, this dinner is great. I am such a good cook. I am awesome." I do this all the time. I even tell other people how awesome I am. Of course, you have to be careful that you only say that to people who really know you. You can't just walk up to someone in the store and say, "I am awesome."

You have to promote yourself in your own mind and occasionally with other people. Don't be conceited and don't be condescending, but do be one hundred percent confident in yourself. You can do anything that you choose to do. You just have to figure out exactly what you want to do. Prioritize what is most important, and do it.

Build up your kids too. Tell them how great they are. Make sure they believe it. Don't wait for a special moment to do this. Just out of the blue, at random times, say, "you are really awesome, I love you." If you have never said it before, they may look at you like you are weird, but that's ok. Just keep doing it. It's your job to make sure your kids have confidence. The more confident they are, the more assertive they will be. Not passive, not aggressive, but assertive.

Tell other people how great your kids are. If the kids can hear you, that's even better. Sometimes they believe it more when they hear you telling other people. Don't ever tell other people that your kids are bad. Don't ever talk down about your kids to other people, especially in front of your kids. This can kill their confidence. It won't make them behave better. If anything, it will make them behave worse. If you don't like their behavior, speak to them privately. But ALWAYS promote them publicly. Yes, it is important that they are well behaved, but it is more important that they are confident in themselves and that they know that you love them, no matter what they do. When they know you love them, no matter what, it helps build their confidence. They know that you accept them, even when they make mistakes. Because they know they are loved and accepted, they will behave better. When they hear you telling other people how wonderful they are, they will try to live up to that image that you are promoting of them.

While you are promoting yourself and your kids, promote other people too. When was the last time you told a co-worker they were doing a good job? The simplest little statements delivered in a positive manner can make a person's day. What about your waitress? When was the last time you told her she was doing a good job? Every day, these people go to work and they are constantly around people and constantly doing things for other people. When was the last time they really felt appreciated? Step outside of your comfort zone and let someone know that you appreciate them.

Build your confidence, build your kids' confidence, and let people know that you appreciate them. Tell people they are doing a good job.

Respect

If we want people to respect us, we have to respect them. "Respect" is one of those tricky words that was probably over-used when you were a child. Sometimes the word makes people defensive. "Why should I respect him?" and "They have to EARN my respect." When I was a teenager, I automatically rebelled at the mere mention of the word "respect." I didn't really understand what it meant, though. It was just one of those words that adults always said when you were in trouble. "Show a little respect." "Respect your elders." Part of my problem was that I didn't feel like I was being respected, so I didn't see any reason to respect other people. That is completely logical to the teenage mind and to some adults as well.

What I didn't realize then is that you have to respect EVERYONE. Not just adults or "your elders." I think also, a lot of adults don't realize that they have to respect kids as well.

When you respect someone, you acknowledge that their opinion matters. You acknowledge that they have a right to an opinion. Their opinion is just as important as your opinion. Their needs, wants, hopes, and dreams are just as important as yours. It doesn't matter how old they are.

How can you expect a person to respect your needs, wants, hopes, dreams, and opinions, if you don't respect theirs? Maybe you are the "official decision maker" in your family. Sometimes there needs to be an official decision maker (both parents working together to make a decision). But that doesn't mean that the kids' opinions don't matter. **If you don't respect them when they are little, then when they are older, they won't respect you.**

Mental self defense

It's easy to let other people affect our happiness. In fact, that is what comes naturally to most people. While it is understandable that sometimes things happen that will upset you, you can't let it control your life. Your happiness is NOT dependant on other people. Your happiness comes from within YOU. When something happens to upset you, deal with the problem and then move on. Don't dwell on it for days. Acknowledge that it upset you and then move on. Is it really worth as much time as you are putting into it?

Your inner happiness and peace are something to be cherished. Don't let other people control that. Don't gossip. Don't listen to gossip. Stay away from it. It will just bring you down.

It doesn't matter what anyone else thinks about you. Just keep doing what you know is right. Check yourself. Make sure it's right. If it is, keep moving forward. Even when you are trudging through mud, don't stop. Just keep moving forward.

Surround yourself with the right people. Surround yourself with people who are like-minded and who do not bring you down. Find people who support your goals and dreams. Be sure to also support their goals and dreams. This is not one-sided. Helping others helps you.

Make a Plan

Figure out what is important in your life. Realize that there are more things in life than what goes on at your school or your job. Think BIGGER! Think OUTSIDE of the box. Don't accept that you have any limitations. Limitations are all in your head. There are no limitations except what you have created. What do you REALLY want to do? What do you REALLY want to be?

When you are thinking about what you want to do or be, go ahead and consider what other people want you to do or be. Write it down. Is that what you want? Do you want to be what other people want you to be? If so, that's ok. Just be honest with yourself.

Think like this:

• If I could do anything in the world that I want to do, what would I do?

• If I could be anything that I want to be, what would I be?

• If I could change anything, what would I change?

Really think about these questions. Write them down. Write only one question on each page. Then write your answers below each question. Use as many pages as you need.

There are no limits. You are brainstorming. So write down everything, even if it seems unlikely. Don't consider the cost of anything. Don't consider the likelihood of it happening. Just write it down.

STOP NOW AND GO DO THAT. DON'T WAIT. DO IT NOW.

Did you do it? How many pages do you have? Now sit down and look at these pages and figure out how to get it done. Research it. See how other people did what you are trying to do. Exactly what steps did they take to get where they are? How can you apply that to your life? Don't say that you can't because I know that you can.

Set Goals

Set goals for your future. No matter what it is that you want to do, you need to set goals. Whether it is for your job, your education, or yourself, set goals.

Decide to make yourself a better person. Figure out exactly what it is about yourself that you want to change and change it. If you want to become more outgoing and assertive, make that your goal. Figure out exactly what you need to do to accomplish that goal, and work towards it.

Make a list of all of the character traits that you want to have and decide how to reach that goal.

Set goals for your education. Do you want to have a formal education?

Where are you now? Do you want to go to college? What is stopping you? There Is no time like the present. Don't wait for that perfect moment to come along where you consider it a good time to go to college. The "perfect time" will never come. There will always be some reason why you think you should put it off. If you have young kids, you will think that you should wait until they are in school. If they are older, you will think you should wait until they are out of school. Don't wait around until you have more money. You will never really feel like you have enough money that you can just quit working and go to school.

Stop making excuses. If you ever thought about going to college and that is what you want to do, just do it. Decide on a college and call an advisor. They will walk you through the financial aid process if you are using financial aid. They will also help you figure out what kind of degree that you want. Go online and look at their website. They are sure to have a list of degrees available.

If you think that you wouldn't have time to go sit in a classroom, look at what online classes they offer. A lot of colleges are offering online classes now. Some colleges are completely online. If you want it badly enough, you will do it. You will find the time instead of finding excuses.

If you decide that you don't want a formal education, that's ok. But there are still plenty of things that you need to learn. Educate yourself.

Always work towards improving yourself.

Set goals for your career. Where do you see yourself in two years? What about five years and ten years? Get a notepad and write down exactly where you want to be in the next few years. Leave spaces between each one so that you can write down how you are going to get there.

Be realistic. This is your future we are talking about, so get real and get with the program. Don't write down things like "win the lottery." Although that would be great, that doesn't need to be one of your goals because you have no control over that other than buying the ticket. So go get a paper and a pen, get serious, and write down what you want to do, and then figure out how to do it.

Every person has a specific set of skills that makes them uniquely qualified to handle certain problems. Figure out what your skills are and then figure out which problems you can fix with your skills. Then go do it.

Perseverance

Once you decide on what you want to do, stick with it. Don't give up because it is too hard or it will take too much time. What are you doing with your time anyway that you can't use it to promote your own goals? So you don't have time to study in the evening because you would rather be watching TV? How is watching TV going to benefit your future?

Yes, you will get tired. You will be worn out and sometimes even get burnt out. But you need to keep reminding yourself of your goals and remind yourself of why you set those goals to begin with.

Double check every once in a while to make sure that you are still on track. Don't be afraid to change it up a little if you get into your goal and realize that you would like to take a different road. Just keep moving forward. Stay in motion.

Focus

Focus on your goals. Focus on the long term and the short term. Whatever it is you are doing, make sure you give it your complete attention. Whether you are talking to someone or working, half of your attention is not what is required.

If you are talking to someone, you are insulting them by not giving them your full attention. I think it is especially important to really focus on what your kids are saying to you, no matter how old they are. In fact, the younger they are, the more important it is to really focus on what they are saying because they aren't always able to fully communicate what they are trying to say. It is up to you as their parent to read between the lines and figure out exactly what they are saying. Don't just brush it off when they are trying to talk to you. If you don't listen to their little problems, they won't bring their big problems to you.

If you are working, you are insulting yourself by not giving it your full attention. Everything that you do deserves your full attention.

If you have problems focusing, set aside a certain amount of time to only do one task. For example, for fifteen minutes don't do anything except paperwork. When that time is up, keep working on it to see how long you can stay focused. This will help improve your focus.

Meditation helps to improve focus. Meditation clears your mind and allows you to be able to focus on only one thing. Meditating for a few minutes just before you start a project can help you focus on it. There are no exact positions for meditation. Get comfortable. I like to put my hands in my lap with my palms facing up because I feel like it helps to draw positive energy into my body. Once you are comfortable, just focus on relaxing each part of your body, one part at a time.

Reading helps to improve your focus because it makes you concentrate on one thing at a time. Cut back on television and increase your time spent reading.

Cut down on clutter. Clutter distracts your mind and affects your ability to focus. Your surroundings should be organized, uncluttered, and serene. Clutter also wears you down mentally and causes you to become frustrated more easily. Organize your space so that you don't get distracted with little things like finding a pen.

Avoid excess distractions, like talking to your friends online or texting, when you are trying to concentrate.

Try to save your texting and online talking for after work.

Follow routines. Get plenty of sleep. If you haven't done so already, read my other book, "A Time for Everything," which discusses setting up routines so that you can get everything done that you need to do and still have time left over.

Make "To-Do" lists. Write how long each task will take. Following a "To-Do" list will help you concentrate. As you mark things off of your list, you will see what you have accomplished and what you need to do next, instead of drifting from one task to another.

Prioritize. Work when you are feeling most motivated and energetic. I focus easier in the mornings. Save the tasks that don't require much thought for the times when you have a problem concentrating.

Plan short breaks. Bursts of activity with short breaks are more productive than forcing yourself to "work" without any breaks. I find that when I force myself to work, that is when I am most likely to instead sit down and surf the Internet. Surfing the Internet is probably not a part of your job description. It would be better to go take a break during that time. Walk away from the computer.

Use your breaks productively. Get some fresh air. Get a drink (not alcoholic), or exercise for a few minutes.

If you work in a noisy environment or if you are distracted by your co-workers, consider getting some earplugs or noise cancelling headphones. Silence can be such a blessing and very soothing. Learn to appreciate silence.

Ground yourself

Learn to ground yourself. Focus on the "now." Instead of rehashing the past or worrying about the future, focus on what is going on in your world right now at this moment.

Pay attention to the world around you instead of just getting caught up in your own thoughts. It's easy to forget to listen to the birds or the wind. FEEL things. Feel the air on your face and the rain on your skin. Focus on these little realities to ground yourself.

Attitude

If you expect to fail, you will fail. If you expect to succeed, you will succeed. You have to work for it. You can't just expect to succeed and then sit around waiting for it to happen. I remember hearing someone say, "as smart as we are, you would think we wouldn't be sitting around here with no money in our pockets." I immediately thought, "well that's the problem...you are sitting around talking about it instead of actually working." You have to put forth the effort. When you first start a project, it will take more work. You have to spend extra time getting it started and set up. Once it is set up, it won't be as much work.

Decide what you are going to do and then do it. Don't accept it when people say it is impossible. What they mean is, "it could be challenging."

Be persistent. Try every single method available to you to solve a problem. When you use up all of those methods, go find some more methods, or create some new methods. Persistent people pick up where everyone else gave up.

Self-discipline

The key word here is "self." Don't try to discipline others into your way of thinking. Our focus should be on fixing ourselves. Our kids will learn by our example.

It will always be easier to take the day off and spend it watching TV or reading a book. But what will you remember tomorrow? Tomorrow will you appreciate that you spent the day doing nothing? Maybe you will. Is it something to write in your journal about? "Today I spent the day watching TV." Then the next weekend..."Today I spent the day watching TV." And the next weekend..."Today I spent yet another day watching TV."

While it is important to have down-time, why not do something else on your day off? Work in your garden or take your kids to the park, or go for a walk. I know there are things that you have wanted to do with your day off that do not involve turning on the television. Why not make a list of those things and start doing them?

I know, it's your day off and you are tired. The more active you are on a regular basis, the more energy you will have.

Get out and make memories. Make something that you would want to write about in your journal. If you don't have a journal, this would be a good reason for you to start one. Having a journal helps you realize what you do with your life. It can help you see what you are spending most of your time doing.

Use it to make lists of things that you want to do. Then use it to write about when you did those things. Do things that you can "write home about." I know that we don't really "write home" much anymore. We have social media, so everyone sees what we do on an hour to hour basis. Sometimes we share too much, but that is a whole other story. But back in the day...when we did "write home," we would write about the things that we had been doing in our lives and what had been going on around us. If nothing had been going on, we either wouldn't write, or the letter would be really short. So think about it, figure out what you would write home about. Have you done anything lately to write home about? If not, maybe you should.

Percentage rule

Generally speaking, ninety percent of the work that you do gets done in ten percent of your time. The other ten percent of the work that you do takes up ninety percent of your time.

I recently recovered a sofa in my house. It is the first time I have ever recovered a sofa. Most of the work was just sewing straight lines. But then there are the tops of the arms, right at the front on the curve. Three sides have to come around and meet each other at this point. I spent most of my time trying to make those curves look right.

Sometimes you have to spend that time on the details. Sometimes you don't. Figure out when you don't have to do the details that take up so much time. If you could just do ninety percent of the work and then outsource the rest of it, you would save a lot of time. If the small details don't really matter, don't do them. Or save them until last.

Your time is one of your most valuable assets. Don't give up quality, but figure out when those little details don't really matter.

FINISH WHAT YOU START!!!!

Seriously, this is a huge pet peeve of mine. Such a simple rule. Just finish what you start. I really don't understand NOT finishing what you start. Say you have five projects going on. You get halfway through each project and then you stop. You have invested a lot of time in those projects. But you wasted your time because they aren't finished. So it's actually like you didn't do anything at all. You can't mark it off your list, so it's not finished.

You are at your desk with a stack of papers, all needing filed. You sit there for hours going through this stack of papers, sorting them out into different piles. Here are all the electric bills, here are all of the gas bills, and here are all of the work orders. So eventually, this huge stack of papers is sorted into all of these smaller stacks of papers. Your idea is that you can then take each stack of papers and file them into the file cabinet. Great idea. Except you stop. You get distracted with something else. So then your desk looks like a tornado hit it. You come back and the mess is driving you crazy, so you grab all of these stacks of papers and put them all together, thinking that you will finish filing them later. Of course then that stack of papers gets more papers on top of it. Then you have to find a certain paper, so you go digging through the pile of papers, disorganizing it again. You have just managed to undo hours of work because you never finished the job to begin with.

Make a list. If you can't mark it off the list, you are not done with it. But don't mark it off until it is finished. FINISH THE JOB.

It may seem like this contradicts my previous statement about the 90 percent rule. It doesn't. Here's why: you have to learn to recognize when a job is "finished." There can always be more details added later and more improvements can always be done to any project. But the project is still "finished."

Take that sofa that I was recovering, for example. I never did make the tops of those arms look exactly like I wanted them to look. But the job is finished because I am satisfied with it. It's not bugging me because I have let go of that obsessive perfectionism that sometimes controls us in these types of situations. Now, if I wanted to get technical, I could get my mother-in-law to come in and fix the tops of those arms. But I am not going to do that because I am satisfied with the results and I know that when someone looks at the sofa, they see a good job. In order to see those little details, they would have to get down on their hands and knees within two inches of the arms. Why would anyone do that? And if they do that...they have problems and need to find something better to do with their time.

So recognize when the job is actually finished.

Working together

Every day, do something to make your life better. Do something to make the lives of your loved ones better.   Work together towards a goal.

My dad had a really big family. He always said that if his family could have learned to work together, they could have owned half of Texas. That's a pretty lofty goal. But look around you.   Who can you work with? Maybe you can just find one person that you can work with. Then maybe you can add one person to that. If it is your family, that's great. If not, that's OK too. Find people who have similar values as you do. Start slow, doing small projects together. Be fair. Work with them as much as they work with you.   Or you may want to start out by doing fun things together.

If you can do the fun things together, maybe you can do some work together.

This was hard for me because I am such a loner. I want to do everything on my own. I don't like asking for help. I had to learn to ask for help before I get overwhelmed.

I also had to learn to let go of some of the control in order to allow people to help me. Just because I am capable of doing it on my own does not mean that I should do it on my own.

I think for a while, I had to prove that I could do everything myself, without any help from anyone else. I had the motivation to do that. I didn't want to "need" anybody. If I did everything on my own, I didn't need anybody.

Once I finally proved to myself that I was capable of "doing it on my own," that's when I decided that it was okay to let other people in to help me just a little. Still, I tend to stand ready to jump in and take over whenever I need to.

I think it is important to BE ABLE to do things on your own, to not depend on other people. I would not want to depend too heavily on anyone. When you depend on someone too much, you make yourself vulnerable. If you suddenly didn't have that person to depend on, what would you do? And it's not really fair to the other person that you depend on them so much. What if they have something better to do?

It is all about balance. You shouldn't have to "do it all on your own," and you shouldn't have to depend completely on someone else. Do whatever you can for yourself. Be willing and able to take care of your responsibilities, whether it is at your job or your home. But also be willing to step back and let other people take some of the responsibility off of you. At home, your kids might start to take over some of your responsibilities. At work, maybe you can learn to delegate and just keep the tasks for yourself that are the most important to you.

Business Leadership-Focus on the good

Don't try to mold people into something that they have no talent for. I really do believe that anybody can learn anything. But you have to recognize the talent of individuals and focus on the talents instead of teaching them a new thing.

If you focus on what they are good at, they can develop that about themselves and they can become better at it. You wouldn't call an accountant to fix your air conditioner and you wouldn't call a repairman to fix your books. Maybe the accountant has a secret talent for fixing air conditioners and maybe that repairman has a secret talent for accounting, but that is not their specialty. Let them do what they are good at. You will get a lot more bang for your buck if you put people into positions that they are suited for

I forget where I read it, but the concept has always stuck with me:

FOCUS ON WHAT YOU DO WELL, AND THEN OUTSOURCE THE REST.

Feed Your Obsessions

If you are obsessed with a person to the point where you are stalking them, I gotta tell you to STOP RIGHT NOW! But, if you have other obsessions, hobbies, or passions, that is what you need to feed.

Years ago, when I was homeschooling my kids, I realized that whatever they were interested in at the time is what they were most easily able to learn. So when they were interested in learning Math, they learned Math. When they were interested in Science, they learned Science. I didn't force them to do handwriting when they wanted to learn to multiply. Whatever they wanted to learn, while they were wanting to learn it, they would soak it up like a sponge. If they weren't interested, they might go through the motions, but it wasn't really sinking in to their heads. Because this is the way I taught them, once they started public school, they were several grade levels ahead on their math. They were not behind on any subject, but they were way ahead on Math. To this day, they are really good with Math.

This same concept applies to anything that you want to learn...anything that you are passionate about or interested in at the time. So whatever it is that you are interested in, feed that interest, that obsession, that passion, and see where it will lead.

Sometimes I become really interested in a subject and I research it and I learn everything that I can possibly learn about the subject. I may have no idea what I am going to do with the information at that time. But I keep learning it until it feels like my head is stuffed full of information and my mind is racing. I get really excited about the subject. Sometimes I can barely sleep because I am so excited about a subject. Then, when I have stuffed my head completely full, I stop and give it a few days to process. I let all of the information absorb completely into my brain. It fills up the corners and settles into exactly the places that it needs to go. Slowly I realize...."Okay, that is where this information goes, and this is what I need to do with this information." I absolutely love learning new things and then taking those things and applying them into other aspects of my life.

I think it's important that we never stop learning. You hear that statement so much now, it is almost meaningless. But once you get in and you start actively pursuing learning new things, exactly the things that you are interested in, you see why it can be so exciting. Maybe when you were in school, you didn't really enjoy it. And maybe that is because when you wanted to learn Math they were teaching Social Studies. I loved college and I learned a lot. But there were so many times in college that I wanted to work with one subject and learn more about that subject, but I couldn't do it because I had to spend my time on a different subject to get done with my homework. But after college, that's when I really felt like I was able to open my mind and learn a lot more things. I could focus on whatever I was interested in. Because I was interested in it, my brain was a sponge for the information.

Don't Limit Yourself

I mentioned previously that you should focus on what you are good at and outsource the rest. I mentioned that you wouldn't call an accountant to do the job of a repairman or a repairman to do the job of an accountant. That being said, DON'T LIMIT YOURSELF. If you are interested in learning to be a repairman or an accountant, DO IT. Even if you are really slow at it at first. You will get faster with it. Just because you are good at one thing, doesn't mean you can't do other things. Of course, if you force it, it won't work. If that accountant has no interest in fixing things and that repairman has no interest in accounting, you are wasting your time trying to fit someone into a mold where they can't utilize all of their abilities. But if they want to learn the subject IN THEIR SPARE TIME, then let them do it. You never know when that interest will turn into a hobby, that hobby into a passion, and that passion into a talent that far surpasses whatever they did before.

I fix computers and I am really good at it. That is my thing. It was a hobby and then a passion and now it is just a part of me. But that doesn't mean that I can't do other things. And it is important that I do other things. For my own peace of mind, I have to know that I can do more than one thing. So when I have time, I am helping my husband fix appliances. I like that sort of thing because it is like a puzzle. But I also like sewing, crafts, painting, home improvements, any kind of construction, woodworking, mud work, organization, and about a million other things. I'm pretty sure I will never be a carpenter, but I am not afraid to jump in and start nailing some boards together. An actual carpenter can do it better than me, but how am I going to learn if I don't jump in and do it. So since I am interested in it, why not do those kinds of things in my spare time? What else am I going to do? Sit around and watch TV?

Leadership Through Service

There is this common misconception that people who serve are beneath people who lead. I disagree. I think that people who serve are the leaders.

We often think of a leader as some big, powerful guy in a suit that sits upstairs in his office yelling at people and pointing them the direction he wants them to go. By definition, that is not what a leader is. A leader is someone who leads. In order to lead, you have to be going somewhere or doing something. Not just sitting there yelling at people and telling them to do things your way.

A good leader will come down out of his office and get on the floor with people, roll up his sleeves, and get to work. He's not afraid of getting his hands dirty.

To be a good leader, people have to follow you because they want to follow you, not because they are afraid of not following you, or they are afraid of getting fired if they don't follow you.

A good leader will start working and encourage others to follow him...not demand it.

A good leader serves. The best example of this is parenting. We know as parents that we are the boss. But every day, we serve our kids. When they are babies, we change their diapers and make their bottles; we feed them, dress them, comfort them, and rock them to sleep. Everything we do is in service to them.

We work to get money to buy them food and clothing and to give them a place to live and pay the bills. Again, this is us serving our kids.

We don't do it because we expect anything in return. We do it because we love our kids and we are responsible for them.

But we are also the boss, or the leader. Just because we do these things to serve them does not make them the boss.

When I cook dinner, I place the food in the middle of the table. Sometimes I have everyone (my husband and my kids) serve themselves and sometimes I serve it for them. That does not make me their servant or inferior to them in any way. I serve them because I created this meal for them and it brings me pleasure to place it before them.

When I clean my house, it is not because I am the servant. It is because I want my family to live in a clean environment and I do not mind serving them in this way so that I may bless my family. Having a clean house helps them feel peace and love. This is a small thing that I can do to show that I love them. Don't get me wrong, I am not up buzzing around cleaning while everyone else is sitting around doing nothing. They each have their chores to do. But I am not going to act like a martyr if I do the majority of the work in the house. That wouldn't be showing love. That would show that I am cleaning because I have to, not because I want to.

Attitude of Servant

Be humble. We are servants to our kids. We don't "Lord" over them. But we are still in charge. We can lead and still have a servant's attitude. How about asking your employees or your kids what you can do to help them with their job or their chores?

Jesus had a servant's attitude. Most people agree, though, that he is an awesome leader. People follow Him because they love Him and they want to be like Him. They believe that His way is right.

Let me interject here that if the only reason you are following Jesus is because you want a reserved seat in Heaven, you might want to go back to church or do a little independent studying and soul searching.

Following Jesus should have nothing to do with what you will receive in return. It shouldn't be because you are afraid of punishment. You should be following Him because you believe that He is right and His way is the right way. You should follow Him because He is good and because you want to be like Him. You should be good for the sake of being good, not just because you want a reward for it or because you fear going to Hell. If you do it for the reward or out of fear, it is not genuine. You think He won't know the difference?

Necessary Motivation

Sometimes motivation is born out of necessity. When a mother suddenly becomes the only income to provide for her children, that is pretty motivating. You know that if you don't get up and go to work, you won't be able to pay your bills and then you will have no utilities. You can't pay your rent, so you will be homeless, or you can't buy food to feed your children. That is pretty motivating.

When I was in this position, I had a regular 40 hour a week job making minimum wage. If I never missed a day of work, I could pay my bills. If no emergency ever came up, I was fine.

It was during that job that I met my husband. He had kids and I had kids and we were pretty adamant about keeping our finances separate.

Then I got laid off, and I wasn't fine anymore. I had a limited number of months' worth of unemployment benefits. I was looking all over the place for a job and I wasn't able to find anything.

I had a hobby though, which was building computers. Of course, I didn't have the money to buy computer parts, but I had a friend who built computers in another town who believed in me. I went to see him one day and he suggested I take some of his computer parts and put them together and sell the computers. Once I sold the computers, I could pay him for the parts. He had known me for a while and he trusted me because he knew that I was honest and wouldn't take advantage of him. So I took enough parts for five computers. I brought them home and put them all together. But then I needed a way to sell them so I had a yard sale. I talked to a lot of people around town and put up fliers and generally started putting the word out. I hadn't lived in my town for very long, so I didn't know a lot of people.

Once people saw that I had a few computers for sale, they started asking if maybe I could fix the computers that they already had. I told them I would give it a try. I figured if I could build them, I should be able to fix them too. So I started doing that a little at a time.

It just took a few months for me to outgrow my house that I was working out of. So I started looking around for some space that I could rent, just a corner in a building somewhere that I could put my computers up for sale and maybe get a few in to fix.

I ended up finding a small building that I could buy instead. I talked to my (future) husband about it to see if he wanted to do it with me. He also fixes things on the side, like appliances so I figured that between the two of us, maybe we could manage to keep the bills paid at the shop and then still have money to pay the bills at each of our homes.

It was kind of a big jump and looking back, I guess it was more like a leap of faith. I just figured that as long as I could make minimum wage at this job, I would be OK. I would have job security because I wasn't going to fire myself.

Even when I was working at one of those jobs where you make an hourly wage, it didn't feel right. No matter how hard I worked, I would make the same amount of money. I could laze around and work slowly, or I could work at full speed. It didn't matter. I made the same amount of money. I could do a really good job or I could do a really crappy job, and it didn't matter because I would get paid the same amount of money.

Of course, I didn't do a crappy job because it just wasn't in my nature. I always believed that everything you do, you should do the very best job you can do at it. Give 100% every single time. Still, it was incredibly annoying to watch the people around me slacking off and making the same amount of money that I did.

That's part of why I enjoy working for myself. I see results. If I work harder and faster, I can make more money. If I slack off, I make no money. It's not for everyone. A lot of people like to know that they can show up at work five days a week and they will have enough money to pay the bills. I understand that. They need the security of knowing that their bills will be paid as long as they show up for work.

If all I do is just "show up" at work, I may not get my bills paid.

I also need to see that I have a potential to make more money if I work harder. My dreams don't fit inside of a box. They don't fit in an "hourly wage."

There was one job I had where I thought that I might be able to advance. Work hard, get promoted, make more money, and all of that. I started asking for more responsibilities. I asked to be transferred to the department that I wanted to be in. They would occasionally put me over in that department.

Then one day the boss called me into her office. I've never been clear what motivated her to do this. We talked about the things I was capable of doing. We talked about my education (which wasn't necessary for the job that I had). We talked about how I had asked to be transferred into another department.

Then she informed me that there was only so far that I could go in this job. She said that I wouldn't get any promotions. And then she said, "You can't have my job, so there is only so far you can go."

I thought it was really strange that she thought I wanted her job and felt it necessary to inform me that it wasn't happening. Having her job had never crossed my mind.

But talking to her made me face the reality that even though I was putting everything that I had into that job, I wasn't going anywhere. I was spinning my wheels.

So I stepped back and refocused and started doing all of my computer stuff on the side, in my "spare time."

I put "spare time" in quotes because nobody really has "spare time." You have to carve out that space of time from the time that you already have. Everyone has the same amount of time. You just have to decide how you want to use yours. That is covered in my other book, "A Time for Everything."

About "hourly wage"

Don't get me wrong, there is really something to be said about making an hourly wage. It does take a lot of will power and discipline. You go to work day after day for the same exact amount of money. But you always know you will get that amount, so you can plan where to spend it. You don't have the ups and downs that you have when you work for yourself. You don't have the surprises. You know that you can pay this bill, that bill, and the other bill, and still have money left to put into savings for "emergencies." When you work for yourself, you have more "emergencies." Like, "Oh, I didn't do as much business this week, and my electric bill is due, so I will take money from my emergency fund." So yes, I do understand and admire people who work for an hourly wage. I just think that it's not for everyone, just like owning a business is not for everyone.

I see both sides of the coin. My dad always had his own business and he had the potential to make a lot of money. He didn't always. He might make a lot of money one week and then not make anything for several weeks.

My mom, on the other hand, makes an hourly wage. That hourly wage is "regular," so she knows exactly how much money she will make and can plan accordingly.

Of course, neither way is right or wrong. They are just right or wrong for certain people. I can't even imagine my dad making an hourly wage. And I can't imagine my mom being okay with not having the security of an hourly wage.

What matters is what each person can handle. There has to be a variety. Not everyone can own their own business and not everyone can work for an hourly wage. If everyone had their own business, there would be no people to work in the businesses.

I do think, though, with any business, you have to give your employees the potential to improve. I think it is human nature to want to make things better. That part of human nature is stronger in some people. If you give them a chance to move up and to progress, it can only benefit the company. The more your employees push to succeed, the more your company will succeed. They push to climb the ladder and, in so doing, they push you further up the ladder too. If you resist, they might push you off the ladder and you may fail. But if you let them push you up, you both succeed. They are happy, you are happy, and your company is successful.

Don't think of it as working yourself out of a job. Maybe they do eventually take over your duties. But that just means that you are freed up to do other things. Maybe you are freed up to grow the company more.

Everyone is good at something. So focus on what you are good at. Let your employees focus on what they are good at. If everyone does what they are good at, you will be successful.

Conclusion

To be successful, you must start from the inside and work outward.

First, you must set a goal, so that you know where you are going.

Second, you must be motivated to attain that goal.

Third, you must have confidence in yourself. You must be assertive. No matter how motivated you are, you must still be assertive in order to attain that goal.

You must have a good attitude, stay focused, discipline yourself, and persevere. Find your passion, your obsession, and feed it.

Don't put limitations on yourself. If you can fully picture it in your head, as many details as possible, you can accomplish it. Just work on making each of those small details happen a little at a time.

Bonus Book:

Controlling Your Emotions-

Be the Boss of Your Own Emotions

Introduction

I really feel like controlling your emotions is something that should be taught in school, from Kindergarten on. Unfortunately, most of us have to learn it through trial and error, and some of us never learn it.

Wouldn't it be nice if we could have complete control over our emotions at any given time? How many times do you look back and think... "Wow, if I hadn't been so angry, I would have said this..." Or you get in an intense emotional situation and instead of sounding logical and convincing, you start crying?

In this book, I will attempt to show you how to control your emotions, instead of letting your emotions control you. I am not a Psychologist and I do not have a degree in this. I am a Mom who makes every effort to study subjects such as this in order to teach them to my kids and make their lives a little easier than mine was.

Take responsibility for your emotions

The very first thing you should learn is that your emotions are *your* responsibility. Your spouse, your girlfriend, your boyfriend, your friends, your parents, kids, brothers, sisters... none of them are responsible for your emotions. They are yours and yours alone. No matter what they do, no matter how bad it is, it is not their fault that you are angry or jealous or emotional in any way. Those emotions come from within you, not from outside of you. So stop blaming other people. "If he hadn't done this, I wouldn't be so angry...." "If they would just stop doing this all the time...." "She said this, or she looked at me like that...." STOP BLAMING OTHER PEOPLE.

First of all, a lot of it is just your imagination. Maybe they didn't even realize how they looked at you. Or maybe they did. Maybe they didn't know that what they said or how they said it would make your blood just start boiling in anger. Maybe they didn't even know you cared about that subject. But even if they did know, even if they intentionally said something to make you angry, YOUR ANGER IS YOUR PROBLEM.

I focus on anger because it can be the most damaging to you and to other people. It can ruin relationships and it can ruin your health. When you are angry, your heart rate rises. Cortisol (the hormone that controls stress) decreases. The "fight or flight" response is activated. Your muscles become tense and your digestive process actually temporarily stops. In the long run, anger can lead to more serious health problems, such as headaches, digestive problems, insomnia, anxiety, depression, high blood pressure, heart attacks, and strokes.

That's just how anger affects you personally. What about how anger affects those around you? First, your anger may very well cause their anger. And while their anger is their responsibility and your anger is your responsibility, shouldn't you do everything in your power to keep these negative emotions away from your family and loved ones? Anger can ruin friendships. It can pull families apart.

When you consider all of the negativity associated with anger, why wouldn't you try to control it better?

Identify your emotions

You should try to identify your emotions throughout the day. Are you feeling happy, sad, angry, stressed? It can be difficult to identify your emotions when you are feeling more than one emotion at a time.

Identifying your exact emotions can help you learn how to deal with them. If you are angry or upset about something, identify that and then try to pinpoint exactly what it was that originally caused you to be upset. Writing it down can help. You might consider keeping a journal for this. Write down the emotion that you are feeling and then try to pinpoint where it started. See if you can find a pattern.

Remember to not blame other people for your anger or your other emotions. So, when you are pinpointing what caused the emotion, think about why you felt that emotion.

Was it your insecurity that caused you to feel that emotion? Was it fear? Maybe it is your lack of confidence that caused the emotion.

Other people cannot be blamed for your lack of confidence. While other people can help you become more confident, ultimately, you are responsible for that.

Every single emotion that we have, we are responsible for it. So while other people can do things that cause our anger, it is up to us whether we stay angry or not. While others can do something that causes us to be sad, it is up to us whether we stay sad or not.

It is normal to feel these emotions when other people do things or when life happens. The initial anger or fear or sadness, all of that is normal. But if we linger over those emotions, that is a choice that we are making.

Let go of negative emotions

Wouldn't it be awesome if we could pick and choose which emotions we are going to hang on to? When something happens that causes us to be extremely happy, wouldn't it be nice to be able to hold on to that feeling forever? Well, you can. It is up to you. Take the good and leave the bad.

DECIDE to hang on to positive emotions, such as love, peace, serenity, and euphoria.

DECIDE to let go of negative emotions, such as anger, resentment, jealousy, fear, and depression.

Make a conscious effort to let go of ALL of the bad. And when you feel happiness and peace, memorize those feelings and bring them back to your conscious mind every day.

Choose how you will react

You have a choice about how to react to a situation. There is always more than one way to respond. You can respond with anger or you can respond with peace. There are probably more ways to respond, but basically they fall into the categories of negative responses and positive responses.

Consider the consequences of each response. Is it worth it to react negatively? Will it matter next year? Is it something that is really not a big deal?

Make sure that you are consciously choosing how to react, not just instinctively reacting. Our instincts aren't always right when it comes to dealing with our emotions.

Remember that you don't always have to be right; and even if you are right, other people don't have to acknowledge that you are right. It should be enough that you know in your heart that you are doing the right thing. You are the one who has to live with YOU, so make sure that you can live with yourself.

While we are on that thought, don't try to change other people. You can only change yourself. Others may learn from your example, but they can only change when they are ready to change, not when you are ready for them to change.

Don't be so Defensive!

I will say that again because it is so important. DON'T BE SO DEFENSIVE!!!

Sometimes we have to be defensive because that is what was built into us in order for us to survive. It's all a part of the "fight or flight" theory. If someone or something is attacking you, you either fight or you flee. Most of the time, we don't have to actually fight or flee. We are not cavemen. Still, those instincts are there to protect us against danger or what we perceive as danger.

But it can be overused and when it is, we create stress that is completely unnecessary. When you are overly defensive, part of your brain just kind of shuts down. I'm pretty sure it's the logical part, but I'm not a scientist. When you are angry, your IQ actually drops (seriously, look it up). Being overly defensive is a kind of anger, so it makes sense that your IQ would drop when you are overly defensive.

When that part of your brain "shuts down," you can't hear what is being said. You can't listen to logic or reason because you are too busy being defensive. You can't learn anything new and you can't benefit from any advice. Please, seriously, ACKNOWLEDGE that maybe you don't know EVERYTHING!

Remember that you can learn from anybody. That doesn't mean that they are smarter than you. Even if they are though, it's okay for people to be smarter than you. Be humble. Have confidence in yourself, but be humble and realize that other people have rights to their opinions and sometimes their ideas and opinions may be right and yours may be wrong. Or maybe they can just add to your way of thinking. But if you are always on the defense, you won't learn anything. People who are overly defensive often refuse to consider that they could be wrong or that they might learn from someone else. Remember that you don't have to always be right and people don't always have to agree with you.

When you are confident in your own ideas, you are more comfortable and can relax because you don't feel like you have to justify your ideas to other people. It really is okay for them to disagree with you.

Most people probably aren't out to get you; even family members. And if you genuinely think that they are out to get you, you probably should just stay away from them. You have that right.

Do you ever feel like people just blindside you with their overly defensive attitude? I know I do. It never ceases to surprise me. You would think it would be something that you can get used to. It's not, not for me anyway. And I really don't want to get used to it because if I do, that means that I am constantly stressed and not relaxed.

There you sit, completely calm...you make a casual comment in passing and you are just BLINDSIDED by instant defensive anger. And then it's over until the next time. You don't want to confront that person about it because it will just cause a huge fight and be blown out of proportion. So what can you do about it?

If you are the one being so defensive, you can change that. It's always easier to change yourself. Just identify why you are being so defensive. What is the root cause? Maybe something happened before to make you snap at such small things. Maybe it is fear that is causing you to snap. What are you afraid of?

Deal with the root of the problem. Take deep breaths, walk away (refer back to walk away section). Remove yourself from the situation.

Fill your heart with peace and love so that there is no room for anything else. "Use your powers for good, not evil." It sounds like a superhero quote, but it's really not. There is so much you can do with your life. Why not build up instead of tear down? That way, you have something to show for your life.

But what about when other people are constantly on the defensive? Notice when they are like this. What are they responding to? Will it help to talk to them or will it make it worse? What are the results that you expect to see? If it's just occasional defensiveness, maybe they are just stressed out that day. But if it happens often, to the point that you are disturbed by it, maybe you need to have a talk with them in a non-blaming, understanding way.

Identifying the bad guy

As I mentioned in one of my previous books, "The Power of Positivity," as much as possible you should remove toxic people from your life. They will suck out all of your positive energy and replace it with negative energy, thereby poisoning you. If you can remove them from your life, you will immediately notice a difference in your stress levels.

Most of the time, those toxic people are blatantly obvious. You know who they are, so you watch for them. Sometimes, though, those people are hard to identify. They can be sneaky. They will be perfectly fine one moment and then the next, they are spewing poison from their mouths.

You won't always notice it. And if you don't, you are probably better off. Have you ever noticed how some people's personalities completely change when they get around certain people? Well, you should watch out for those people.

Don't you wish sometimes that life was like the movies where everything was black and white and you always know the good guy from the bad guy? Or like in the old westerns where the good guys wear white hats and the bad guys wear black hats. It was like their team colors. I always kind of wondered if, way back then, they did actually do that. If so, who made that rule and who got to decide what color of hat you wore? I am guessing that was a personal decision. But did they just go into the old mercantile and be like, "Excuse me; this white hat isn't working for me anymore. I think I want to try the black hat."

Then they step out onto the old wooden sidewalks into the dusty streets and this music plays in the background and suddenly everybody knows that he's the bad guy...because of the hat.

I think if I owned that mercantile, I would just refuse to sell those blasted black hats.

Seems to me that if he wanted to be really sneaky, though, he would wear a white hat and everyone would think he was the good guy until.....

BAM!!!

Then he shows his bad guy side and someone says, "Oh hey...that was tricky...I didn't see that coming AT ALL, since he wasn't wearing a black hat!"

Yeah, it's not so easy in real life though. We sometimes have to guess at who the bad guy is. They aren't always obvious. But if you watch and you open your mind, you will know them by their works. And then when they do something completely off the wall, you won't be caught off guard.

While it would be nice to think that we can change them, it is much easier to change ourselves. So yes, talk to them about their behavior if you know them well enough or if you are comfortable with talking to them. But recognize that they may not want to change as much as you want them to change. Or they may not want to change at all. And that is their decision. But then it is your decision whether or not you want them in your life.

Remember when you talk to them to use a calm, peaceful tone of voice. Don't place blame. State your problem. State what you would like to happen. And then that's it. "I perceive this as a problem. This is what I would like to happen." Once they know you see it as a problem and they know what you would like to see happen, It is up to them whether or not to change. Don't get caught up in the blame game. Don't get caught up in long drawn out explanations or excuses. Don't get in an argument. You stated what you perceive as a problem in a calm rational manner. You just need to let that person know that you didn't feel comfortable with his behavior.

Here is an example:

Say that you are an employer and your employee has been disrespectful to you. Ideally, you would deal with that immediately and say, "John, I need you to not talk to me in that manner. I wouldn't speak to you that way, and I expect the same treatment in return." Or maybe you would just say, "John, I need to think this over. I will get back with you on it."

Depending on the circumstances, you would have to alter what you are saying. The point is that you are NOT getting in his face and yelling, "You S.O.B.! You will show me some respect or you are fired!" Or "I am the boss and I deserve respect and I expect you to give it to me." Or "It's my way or the highway, buddy."

Obviously, the second way would really make someone angry and it would not help your case at all. You cannot demand respect. It has to be freely given.

If you do not deal with the problem as it is happening, it becomes a little more difficult. They know you have been thinking about the issue, so in a way, they have had a certain power over you. It may be perceived as a weakness. But talking about it later gives both parties a chance to cool off a little. You can think about it and identify exactly what the problem is and then decide whether or not it is a big enough problem that you need to talk to them. Once you decide to talk to them, do it in a calm, rational manner. If you need to, use a monotone to take the emotion out of your voice. Speak a little more slowly. If you talk too fast, you tend to get a little stressed out, and the other person will also get stressed out. So slow your speech down just a little, and use a calm, soothing voice, almost a monotone. State the problem exactly as you perceive it. "John, I have noticed that you are showing disrespect to me lately. Can you tell me if something is going on that I should know about? Is there a reason that this is happening?" Give him a chance to tell you. Maybe his dog just died or something. There may be a legitimate reason for his behavior. But if it has been just slowly escalating, maybe he has just gotten used to acting like that and he does it more and more without realizing it.

Take Ownership of Your Emotions

Have I already said that? Well it's worth saying again. Take ownership of your emotions. They are your responsibility, not anyone else's.

Just about every emotion that you have is a decision that you made, even if it was subconscious. That doesn't mean that the emotions are not real. They are very real. But you can control them more than you think you can. You have to decide to take control.

Yes, when something happens, we immediately, instinctively, feel certain emotions. But after the initial emotional surge, you need to step back and decide what you want to feel. Do you want to feel anger, sadness, jealously, rage, etc?

Or would you rather feel a more positive emotion.

Take jealousy, for example. That is probably one of the most useless emotions ever created. It takes up so much energy and causes so many problems. It is probably one of the biggest causes of divorce. And it is probably all in your head. And if it's not in your head, will you being jealous change anything?

If you think your spouse is cheating on you, will it help to get jealous? Will it make him or her stop cheating? Probably not. But you being jealous when he or she is not cheating will definitely cause problems.

I see it a lot. People get jealous, thinking their partner is cheating. They get stressed out. They have no proof, so they go looking for proof. Of course, the "proof" won't make them feel better. And is it really "proof"?

If it happens, it happens and you deal with it then. If it doesn't happen, great. But you being jealous might cause it to happen. If you are always accusing your spouse of being unfaithful, he or she may just decide that they might as well do it since you already believe they are doing it anyway. And if you are thinking that they are being unfaithful, you are not trusting them. Trust is a really difficult thing to regain in a relationship. I really think that you not trusting them can cause as much damage as them not being trustworthy.

Why bother? If you really don't trust each other that much, why are you together? "Love, fight, or get your guns," as the old saying goes. I don't mean literally "get your guns," because that wouldn't help at all, I promise.

My point is, you need to make a decision whether or not to trust your spouse. You need to make a decision whether or not to be jealous.

If he or she is actually cheating, you will figure it out eventually and then you can deal with it at that time. But there is no reason to sit around for years worrying about it and creating this stress in your own mind.

Besides that, if your spouse is cheating on you, he or she does not deserve you. So let it go and move on.

Seriously, though, don't just jump to that conclusion. It makes me crazy when I see people automatically jump to that conclusion because they couldn't get their spouse on the phone for over an hour and so therefore, he/she must be cheating. Really? You have such little faith in yourself and your spouse? Hmmm, maybe their phone was turned off? Have a little faith.

Jealously seriously is the most useless emotion ever created. You should get rid of that. Just ban it from your life.

Emotions are okay

Being in control of your emotions is not the same as not having any emotions at all. Our emotions help form our personalities. They make up who we are.

So if you want to change who you are, you can change your emotions. Change the way you look at things, change the way you do things. Change your actions. When you purposefully, intentionally change yourself, you can then shape the person that you want to be in the future. Decide what you want to be "when you grow up," and then set out to make that happen.

It's okay to cry. It's okay to get angry. It is NORMAL to feel emotions. It is not okay to let your emotions rule your life. It is not okay to become so angry with your spouse that you fly into a screaming rage in the middle of the grocery store.

Controlling your emotions is not about making them go away. In fact, in some instances, your emotions can expand.

Open your mind. Open your heart. Feel with your instincts. Feel the power that surrounds you in nature and in our environment.

Once you make your environment into a positive, nurturing

atmosphere, you will feel a greater sense of power within yourself. You won't feel so helpless. You won't feel so much like your world is out of control.

When your environment is positive and nurturing, you can more easily open up your mind and your heart and you can then rise above negative emotions.

You will be able to feel the positive energy surrounding you, and you will treasure that energy. You won't want to do anything to jeopardize the peace that surrounds you and your family.

Therefore, when you start to become angry, jealous, frustrated, depressed, or unhappy in anyway, you will stop yourself because you realize that peace is what you should be seeking. You will realize that if you call what's-her-name on the phone and tell her what you really think of her, it will create a snowball effect that cannot possibly end well.

What would be the point of the confrontation? Would it fix the problem? Chances are that person already knows what you think of her. So calling her up and yelling at her would do...what? Make you look tough? Really? To who?

And then after this yelling match on the phone (or in person), is the problem going to go away? Well, I don't know your situation. Maybe it would. Maybe it would make that person so angry that they never speak to you again. And maybe that is what you want. Or maybe it would just make them angry, make you angry, give you a headache, make your chest hurt, and stress you out. So who won that argument? Certainly not you.

No, you will win the argument by not engaging in it at all. If you really have something to say and you think it is important, here is an idea:

Write it down, type it up, print it out, put it in an envelope, and go down to the post office and send that letter to that person by registered mail. Not by regular mail. Make sure it is registered mail.

If you are willing to do all of that in order to get that information to that person, then maybe it needs to be said. Maybe. Or maybe you don't let go of your anger quickly enough. Sending it registered mail will show you a small part of what it will cost you to get this point across to this person. Maybe if you just sent it regular mail, you would still do it. That would cost you less than fifty cents. But when you have to send it registered mail, you have to think about whether or not it is worth it. That will cost several dollars. I don't work at the post office, but I want to say it's about four dollars to send a letter through registered mail. So, is it worth all of the effort to type it, print it, take it to the post office, and send it registered mail? If it's not that important, then maybe it's not important enough to start an argument over.

If at all possible, instead of listening to someone yell at you, ask them to put it in writing, type it up, print it and send it to you by registered mail. Let them know that you will not answer any other form of communication. Don't answer emails or phone calls or any form of social media. This should cut down on all of the nonsense you have to listen to, and it will also help you learn better how to control your temper.

One more thing to keep in mind...anything that you put in writing can be used against you in a court of law. So think about that before you go writing anything that could get you in trouble.

Of course, most times, our family members would assume that we are being sarcastic if we told them to put it in writing. Someone who lives with you probably won't do that. It works better for people who work with you...people you can walk away from.

Hopefully, anyone who lives with you respects the peace that you so carefully protect in your house, so they won't be yelling at you or in front of you.

But there will always be something. Like those family gatherings where your Great Uncle Dilbert just has to start an argument with your Uncle Frank about the state of the Union. And probably one of them is Democrat and the other is Republican.

Or maybe you made the mistake of discussing politics at a family gathering. Whatever the reasons, it is bound to happen that once in a while you will find yourself in a situation where someone is yelling at you. So what do you do when that happens?

While not always a good thing, in certain situations, emotionally distancing yourself can be beneficial to your well-being. If someone is yelling at you, you have choices in how to handle It.

You could:

- Yell back. (Not recommended)
- Be assertive and tell them that you do not appreciate being yelled at and to please speak to you in a normal tone of voice. (Best choice)
- Distance yourself emotionally.

Distancing yourself can be difficult to learn if you have never done it. Eventually, if you do it enough, it would become second nature

There are some times when distancing yourself from a situation is very helpful. There is a difference between distancing yourself from a situation and distancing yourself from a person. Be careful to pay attention to whether you are distancing yourself from the person or the situation. If you distance yourself from the person, you could start to experience problems with your relationships. Distancing yourself from the situation, though, can help to relieve a lot of unwanted worry and stress.

Here is one form of distancing. This method works when you are in the middle of a stressful situation, such as someone yelling at you.

Block it out. Take a deep breath and think about something else. Go to your "happy place," or think of something logical or unemotional, like naming all of the Presidents of the United States or all of the states. Counting in your head works for some people. Anything with numbers doesn't work as well for me because numbers tend to stress me out anyway. So if I am having a problem blocking someone out, I will begin reciting in my head... "Alabama, Alaska, Arkansas, Arizona...." Then I get to the B's and normally get sidetracked about that time because I always hesitate and think... "Birmingham..." Then I get distracted because I think, "Really? There are no states that start with a B?" So then I tune back in and see if they are still yelling and if so, I continue, "California, Connecticut, (no not Kentucky, that's a K), Delaware, Florida...."

You should try it. I bet you can't name them all. Something like 75% of adult Americans cannot name all of the states. I say "something like" because I can't remember the actual percentage. That's a number and, like I said, I don't do those.

By the time I go through all of this, hopefully whoever is yelling has realized that I am not responding and has therefore stopped yelling. If not, it's probably time to walk away. That's another way to deal with those tense situations. Just walk away. It will annoy them to no end. Have you ever been yelling at someone and they walked away? It irritated you, didn't it?

Later on, consider writing down your feelings in a journal. After all, we don't want to deny them or bury them; we just want to channel them into the direction that we want them to go. It's not good to keep things locked inside, but also it's not always good to lash out and get in that screaming match.

There is also a form of distancing that works for longer term things that are worrying you.

Say that you are trying to get a job. You really want that job. It would be great for your family and you could make more money, etc. But you are so focused on it that you are stressing out about it. You have done everything in your power to get the job, and now you are just waiting. And worrying. And stressing. Well you need to stop. There is nothing that you can do. So put it out of your mind. Distance yourself from the situation. CARE LESS ABOUT IT. It's just a situation. How much does it really matter? Yes, it's important. But in the long run, how much does it matter? And will stressing about it make it any better?

Or what about that loan that you really want? Or that car that you want. You are not sure if you will be able to get it, but you have done everything in your power. Now you are waiting. It's really not up to you anymore, is it? So CARE LESS ABOUT IT. That's basically what distancing yourself is. You care less about the situation, so if you don't get that job, that car, or that loan, you are not devastated. We become devastated when we get our hopes up too high. And we love to get our hopes up high, don't we? We think about how great it could be. We plan what we will do if we get that new job or that new car. We get ourselves worked up over it. We build up our expectations and then if it falls through, we are incredibly disappointed and devastated. We may even sink into depression. But if you didn't care about it so much to begin with, you wouldn't be so hurt and let down if it falls through. Wait to celebrate until after you get the loan, or the car, or the job. Don't plan for it, only to be let down. Whatever it is that you are stressing out about, just back off and distance yourself. Look at it from the outside looking in. Pull yourself out of the situation, care less about the situation, and distance yourself. You will have a lot less disappointment. Don't pin your hopes on one situation. Stop getting your hopes up so high. Get your hopes up AFTER everything goes the way it should.

This book is not about suppressing emotions because that can be bad for your health. Emotions exist in part to help us on a subconscious level to be able to understand what is going on around us that our logical, intellectual mind does not understand. So no, don't suppress your emotions, but rather, control and channel them into a positive direction.

Negative emotions can cause negative health problems. Positive emotions promote healing and happiness, which makes us healthier.

Of course, you will sometimes feel negative emotions. But it is important that you don't allow those emotions to control you, but rather you should control them. Channel them into something positive.

So your boss yells at you. What are you going to do about it? Do you think he was justified? Maybe you have something you need to change. While I believe that yelling at someone is never really the answer to any situation, what point was he trying to get across? Do you agree with that point? Is there something that you need to change? Clearly he needs to change the way he handles situations, but again, you have to worry about changing yourself, not other people.

If you disagree with whatever point he was trying to make (amongst all the yelling), what are you going to do about that? Will it help if he knows that you disagree? Will you get fired? Demoted? Yelled at some more?

Whatever that emotion is that you are feeling, let it motivate you into making positive changes. Whether it is your behavior or your actions that you are changing, or if you will be looking for another job....whatever you decide to do, just do it. Don't sit around waiting for it to change on its own. If you react exactly the same way that you have always reacted, you can expect to get exactly the same results. How dld that work out for you?

As a brief note, be careful of knee-jerk reactions. Don't go quitting your job because you were yelled at. Take time to think. Step back from your emotions, distance yourself from them. Acknowledge them, but don't dwell on them. For example, after your boss yells at you, don't spend hours or days dwelling on it and stressing out. That's not going to fix the situation. Acknowledge the emotions. "I am angry because he said this. I don't believe I deserved that treatment." Of course, if you do think you deserved it, why are you angry about it? Shouldn't you instead be thinking, "Hey, way to go boss! High five! I really deserved to be yelled at and I would have done the same thing if our situations were reversed!" Do you still think you deserved it? You sure? Then like I said, no reason to be angry. But you might want to consider going over the section of passive behavior again.

Deciding to be Happy

Happiness can be either intrinsic or extrinsic, just like with motivation. Whether or not you are happy depends on YOU, not on someone else. YOU are completely responsible for your own happiness. If you depend on other people to make you happy, or if you depend on outside events to make you happy, you will never truly be happy. You will temporarily be happy, until the newness wears off. Then you will be seeking out some new form of extrinsic happiness.

Buying a car may make you happy for a while. Buying a TV may make you happy for a while. But that is an extrinsic happiness and it is not going to last. You have to be happy intrinsically, within yourself, for it to be a lasting happiness.

Most of my life I have been either depressed or on the verge of depression. I would constantly seek out new things to make me happy. But it never lasted long. My first step towards true happiness came a few years ago when I realized the benefit of being positive. I wrote a book on that, "The Power of Positivity." Please read that book, because it leads up to this one.

At that time, I realized that I was torturing myself with my inner chatter. Constantly, I had negative chatter running through my mind. My thoughts were almost always negative. If something wasn't wrong, I would find something that was wrong, no matter how small.

Once I realized that I was bullying myself in this way, I set out to change that. I worked very hard, learning, step by step, to not dwell on negativity. I realized that when I am around people who are very negative, I feel as if I am pulled down. My energy drains away and I end up with a headache.

So I had to work to distance myself from negativity. That helped me to focus more on the positive aspects of my life. I had fewer headaches and much less stress.

That was one of my first steps along my journey.

That was only a first step, though. I learned to be less negative and more positive. I learned to relax a little. I learned to meditate to relieve stress.

That was a huge step for me, overcoming the habit of negativity.

But it still felt like something was missing. Yes, I was more positive. Yes, I was more relaxed and less stressed out, but still there seemed to be something missing. I still seemed to be down in the dumps more often than I should be. For no apparent reason.

That's when I realized that you can just "decide" to be happy. Whatever you want to be...you can just "decide" to do it and then just work to do it. You can figure out a "formula" for whatever it is that you want to feel in your life. If you want to feel calm and peaceful, you can decide to do that and then just set out to make your life like that. Peace and calm are something you feel from the inside, not the outside. All of your feelings come from inside of you and have very little to do with what is going on around you. Yes, those external forces can affect it, but they are not the main reason for you to feel that way.

Feeling calm during a storm

Imagine if you could feel calm and peaceful when someone is yelling at you. Just imagine that. Can you picture it? Someone is standing there yelling at you and yet, you feel calm and peaceful. Well, you can train your mind and your body to do that when you want to do it. I am not saying you should always be calm and peaceful when someone is yelling at you. Sometimes you may want to yell back. Sometimes it may be in your best interest to defend yourself. But sometimes, its not. Sometimes it will just make matters worse.

Imagine someone yelling at you and getting no reaction from you whatsoever. Or getting a calm, peaceful response. How will they react? Most likely, they will begin to calm down. They may even wonder why they are yelling. They may second guess themselves and wonder if what they were yelling at is worth yelling about. After all, if you are not getting upset, maybe they shouldn't be either.

Wouldn't it be great to just be able to use logic? To make decisions based on what we think instead of what we feel. Again, sometimes, you have to let your feelings help you make decisions. That's where basic intuition comes through. But sometimes, we don't want our feelings to influence our decisions. Maybe we don't want to yell at our boss, even if we feel like it, because we know we will probably get fired if we do that. So we learn to control our feelings and emotions. We learn to be separate from our feelings and emotions. We learn to set those feelings and emotions aside and to choose what feelings we want to have. So when we want to be calm and peaceful when someone is yelling at us, we can do that if we choose to.

We can choose calm. We can choose peace and happiness. It takes a lot of willpower until you learn to do it. Eventually, it can become second nature.

Practice on little things. Don't just expect to just right in and be able to feel complete peace in the middle of turmoil.

For example, say someone does something or makes a decision that you disagree with. It can be something small. Whatever small thing that would normally annoy you. When that happens, PRACTICE not getting upset. Use logic on yourself.

Is it worth getting upset about? Will it matter tomorrow or next week or next year? Does it directly affect you personally? If not, why worry about it? And if so, again, how important is it?

Ask yourself if it will do any good at all to argue. Will it change anything? Sometimes it depends on who it is. Will you ever see that person again? If not, how will it help you to argue? Do you think that you will change their life for the better? You probably won't. If it's someone you know, ask yourself if it will do any good to argue. What do you hope to accomplish by arguing? Are you hoping to prove that you are right and they are wrong? Why do you want to do that? Do you think it will make you feel better? How will it make the other person feel? Will the other person actually believe that you are right, or that you are smarter than them?

When you really step back and look at the reasons that you argue, is it worth it? Have you accomplished something great? Do you feel better about yourself? If you know that you are right about something, what does it matter if other people think that you are right? Isn't it enough that you know that you are right? (Assuming that you actually are the one who is right) And is it something that can be proven? Can you go on the Internet or to the library and look up the answer to the argument? Is it black and white? If it can be proven, why are you worried about it? Just tell that person to go look it up on the Internet. Then they will either prove that they are right or you are right. Isn't the Internet great? Shouldn't we be able to solve a lot of arguments with the Internet?

But what about the other arguments? What about the arguments that are more opinions than facts? Those are more difficult because you can't just tell them to go look it up on the Internet. Go back to the question....how important is it? Seriously think about this. What would happen if everything was done the way the other person wants it to be done? Would the whole world fall apart?

Some things are worth arguing over and some things aren't. You have to decide what is worth arguing over and what isn't. What are you willing to "fight til the death" for? I think if you really analyze it, there are probably very few things you are willing to "fight til the death" for. Most of the rest of it doesn't really matter. Even money issues. What is it worth to be right? What will it cost you?

Distance yourself from those things that aren't so important. Money, for example. Yes, you need food, clothing, and shelter to provide for yourself and your kids. But do you really need more than that? How important is it? What are you willing to give up to insure that you have more money? Are you willing to give up time with your family?

Think about what is important to you. Think about what is worth fighting for. Not every little issue is worth fighting over.